The Welcome

T0162347

The

Poems by
David Joel Friedman

Welcome

University of Illinois Press

Urbana and Chicago

1 2 3 4 5 C P 5 4 3 2 1

Library of Congress Cataloging-in-Publication Data

Friedman, David, 1938–
The welcome : poems / by David Joel Friedman.
p.   cm. — (National poetry series)
ISBN-13: 978-0-252-03048-2 (cloth : acid-free paper)
ISBN-10: 0-252-03048-6 (cloth : acid-free paper)
ISBN-13: 978-0-252-07292-5 (pbk. : acid-free paper)
ISBN-10: 0-252-07292-8 (pbk. : acid-free paper)
I. Title. II. Series.
PS3606.R557W45   2006
811'.54—dc22   2005011102

The National Poetry Series

The National Poetry Series was established in 1978 to ensure the publication of five poetry books annually through participating publishers. Publication is funded by the Lannan Foundation; the late James A. Michener and Edward J. Piszek through the Copernicus Society of America; Stephen Graham; the International Institute of Modern Letters; the Joyce and Seward Johnson Foundation; the Juliet Lea Hillman Simonds Foundation; and the Tiny Tiger Foundation. This project is also supported in part by an award from the National Endowment for the Arts, which believes that a great nation deserves great art.

2004 Competition Winners

David Friedman of New York, New York
The Welcome
Chosen by Stephen Dunn; published by the University of Illinois Press

Tyehimba Jess of Brooklyn, New York
Leadbelly
Chosen by Brigit Pegeen Kelly; published by Verse Press

Corinne Lee of Austin, Texas
PYX
Chosen by Pattiann Rogers; published by Penguin Books

Ange Minko of Brooklyn, New York
Starred Wire
Chosen by Bob Holman; published by Coffee House Press

Camille Norton of Stockton, California
Corruption
Chosen by Campbell McGrath; published by
HarperCollins

For Miriam

Contents

Foreword

David Friedman's *The Welcome* persisted in overcoming my
resistances to it. First, there was the issue of the prose poem.
Though it's a form that in many ways appeals to me, I'm wary
that in the wrong hands it can be a vehicle for various indul-
gences, and/or an excuse for the absence of sentence-by-
sentence rigor. And here was an entire book of prose poems!
Second, as readers will quickly realize, the protagonist of
many of these poems is a character called "the green bear."
Normally that fact alone would be cause enough for me to
throw the manuscript across the room.

But *The Welcome* with its green bear kept on insisting on
itself. Increasingly it seemed like Lewis Carroll had joined
forces with Russell Edson, and the synthesis was David
Friedman. "Once upon a time I was once upon a time," he
writes. "Now I am always." And about the green bear's slov-
enliness, we hear, "His vest was in tatters, his stevedore's cap
ruined, and his do-re-mi in disrepair." It is language like this
that kept me returning to these oddly smart poems, and to
their high-risk author. Much like Edson, no apologies here
for the absurd, even the silly. This is my world, Friedman
seems to be asserting, and here it is for your delectation.

The fact is that *The Welcome* is full of pleasures, both lin-
guistic and ideational. There's a philosophical intelligence
behind it, one that will rarely allow itself the sobrieties of the
philosophical. In the title poem, he writes, "Do you wish to

be naturalized in my arms? Let me instruct you in the new tongue. Tread softly; Death too first makes inquiry, then shows the way." That's about as sober as Friedman allows himself to get.

More typically, he blends surreal hijinks with compelling seriousness, as in the conclusion of "Who I Am." "In the sourdough of my creation, I was destined to be the dugout of my dreams: sent downstream, rudderless, stirred by the reeds and the water lilies, to a makeshift harbor and a jerry-built boathouse, wherein the past labors to be renamed, and damned was the middle of the journey."

At their best, an original voice guides a distinctive sensibility in these poems. They'll give you, if you let them, one of literature's underrated virtues: a good time.

Stephen Dunn
Winner of the Pulitzer Prize
for Poetry, 2001

Acknowledgments

Thanks to the following for their love, friendship, and encouragement: Geoffrey Nutter, Luis Francia, Corinne Schlam, James McConkey, Alan and Royce Friedman, and Sejal S. Shah.

The Welcome

Whirlwind

The whirlwind came and carried away his trees and
bushes and plants. It carried away his roof, and the roof of
his silo. It carried away the mailman at his appointed rounds,
and distributed the mail haphazardly. It looked to be an
extended whirlwind, for its energy toiled at the fields and
uprooted the sycamores and scarecrows. The whirlwind
engaged him at the intellectual level, for it fostered the
philosophy of whirlwinds, wherein the rake and the hoe and
other farm implements are carried up into the sky, where
they might toil at the fields of the sky, and be judged.

His house moreover was banished, and his dreams. His
aspiration to be a corsair of the fields. His fortitude in the
midst of snake-like enchantment. This was the chiefest of his
virtues: wherein he plied the same field as the whirlwind,
and coughed up the acidic phlegm of the roughneck storm.
Remote, this storm, from the scalawags, and from the fields,
defenseless.

Dreamer

The green bear was settled in for the winter. His cave was as warm as his haunches. He rested his head on his paws and slept, and began to dream.

In the first dream, the green bear slew his enemies without mercy. In the second dream he was besieged, and barricaded against the knighthood. The last dream was a dream of madness: the green bear bastioned against the elements, and a fiery tombstone.

The green bear wrote down all his dreams on birchbark. In the spring, he went to an analyst. He told her the three dreams. She said, "Sir, you are rumored to be one of the bear family. Pray, tell me, how did you become so green?"

"I became green when a scion was cut from older stock and the cottage trade took hold. Green is the color of the Adirondack, and life," he said, "is a blitzkrieg."

"Then," said she, "allow me to interpret your dreams. In the first dream, you fear a bugbear. In the second dream, you have not properly washed. And in the third dream, nature remonstrates you for being singular. You would do well to close the gap between you and your forefathers."

The green bear paid the analyst for the nifty interpretations, then went about his business. He was glad he had not discussed his amours. A voice at the back of his head told him to rise and shine.

Flugelhorn

Zero, said the deadlock. Habeas corpus, said the matter-of-fact. Old, said the tin pan alley.

With this in mind the sawyer blew out the candle and in the dark rubbed elbows with the carboniferous. And by a shoestring guise he awakened the sentiment of the old confabulator. Please, said the touchstone, touch me. Please, said the touch, a plea. An apple if you will, sir, said the halibut. Until at last it was one fish talking to another, and the bubbles rose to the surface. And the flood huddled in the wings, where the trap was, pulled by horses, spun in a genuine conglomerate of seed; like the scree of a metaphor, when you have hugged and pinched it. Like a flugelhorn.

The Green Bear Shanghaied

The green bear was in the back seat of a car, sandwiched between two goons. He said, "What is this? Where are you taking me? And why?"

A goon in the front seat turned around and said, "Not so fast, green guy. You know why you're here. You have the designs for the new Superpistol, and we want them."

The green bear objected. "Sirs, I am only a middleman. These paws have never touched a Superpistol. The man you want isn't a bear at all, he's a man."

All the goons were listening. The green bear continued, "If I ever had the Superpistol I don't have it anymore. The prototype is in the hands of the law. Laugh it up, gentlemen."

They drove to a deserted farmhouse, where they chained the green bear to a wall and began torturing him.

The first torture was rootlessness: the green bear cut off from his ancestors.

The second torture was denigration: his art maligned.

And for a third torture they offered him fresh strawberry pancakes, with butter and syrup, then withdrew the offer at the last minute.

This last was the worst indignity. The green bear tore and tore at his chains until the farmhouse came crashing down, burying all the goons. The green bear, unlike Samson, survived, and made his way back to civilization, dragging bits and pieces of the farmhouse. He learned that in his absence

Congress had forbidden the construction of the Superpistol as a weapon too horrible to imagine. He was enjoined from further research into the making of the Superpistol.

The green bear found the woman who betrayed him, and plugged her. He continued his adventures.

Altimeter

What is the altimeter of your excellence? Wherein are you childlike, from hunger? Edify yourself; branch out; flow like the cormorant through many weathers. Build a roof over your defile, and shadow-forth your excellence. In a finale, plump for the arcane. So that your five-years' demon descends, to haunt your affect; so that you put no lid on your challenge, but ledger your penmanship. Arise, and sun-bake your poetry; with a push/pull pen, for excellence; in a fusillade, for endeavor.

The Past

I am the past. Stepchild of the future. How is this so?
Feed the flames of my youth, and I will tell. Once upon a
time I was once upon a time. Now I am always. The disasters
of my life burn like watchfires in the night, lighting my way,
giving sporadic warmth. Mama Bear and Papa Bear are no
more. Now am I a child of the sun and the moon, and surro-
gate of the possessed. Affirm my textures; light my cadres;
squire my breviaries. Thus and so I foretell: the past as pred-
ator; the present as nemesis; the future as foothold, victory.

Chef

So the chef concocted this wondrous dish with apples and cherries and sandpipers. So he struggled with the ingredients—to keep it light but substantial. So he tore down the old and upraised the new; crafted his syllogism; and earmarked his transubstantiation.

And then he tried it out. The first customer was a lumberjack. The lumberjack said, "I cannot eat this. This is made of apples and cherries and confections." A fireman said, "I cannot eat this; this dish is made with sandpipers." Finally he asked an old sailor to try it. "Hmm," said Odysseus, "just like home. Now I will bring you with me as my personal chef."

And that is how Odysseus and his men survived their voyage. They fetched the chef each day and demanded only the best. The chef, unfettered, concocted many other rare dishes, which won Penelope over too on the day of reckoning.

Here's to chefs! And especially, here's to sandpipers!

Magda

The choirmaster attended the deathbed of one "Charles," who asked for, and got, the choirmaster's blessing. Then the choirmaster went for a drink.

He had a slug of this and a slug of that. He remembered Charles in his youth. He remembered too a woman named Magda, who had loved both of them years apart. Then he headed for home.

Suddenly he stopped. For there before him on the pathway ahead was Magda, with her dark eyes and raven hair, looking lovelier than ever. After all these years they had forgotten nothing, and they relived the joys of their youth. Months went by. Until at last winter came, with its snowy blasts, and the choirmaster assembled his friends. He told them:

"Friends, it is deafening to be here so quickly. I admire all of you, and admonish the rest: mistake me not. I mean to make Magda my lawful wedded wife."

So the wintry cold came and went, and the choirmaster and Magda donned wet suits and married underwater. But if the tale were truly told, you would wake up one morning with a terrible headache, and your mother, or someone like her, would say, "Blame it all on Magda. Or on Magda and Charles. Or on the witch."

My tale is done. May the snowy blasts of winter prevent trespass, and protect this house.

Heliotrope

Don't wend that way, Mr. Peppercorn; that way is steep. Beware the icicles, Mr. Peppercorn.

Now there came into the possession of Mr. Peppercorn a heliotrope; and he did not know what that was, or what to do with it. So, to seem perspicacious, as well as virile, he enscrolled a pepperbox with the theme of the first icicle, and the theme of the second, and the third, and so on. He beclouded the scene with surface tension, and clenched his teeth like a clavichord. It was audacious, it was hail-fellow-well-met, for Mr. P., a polyglot, wise but obstreperous in his many years.

Dishabille

The green bear was slovenly this day. His vest was in tatters, his stevedore's cap ruined, and his do-re-mi in disrepair. His tie was jaundiced, and his keepsake, a watchfob, obscene. His socks were circumspect, as were his pantaloons. So merrily he leisured his way through his afteryears, slovenly, intact, a prizefight of the emotions; and his watchfob, by the dozens, was fetching in the extreme. This was the riddle of his flight-log, on the dustiest airstrip, where his style was no-account. All these words, by the dozens.

Ladder

I am a ladder. I am drawn up and down; laid lengthwise.
Spot me leaning against a wall. Sketch me propped against a
tree. All but the most fearful try to climb me sometime dur-
ing their lives, and, being sturdy, I do not disappoint them.
My steps are rungs; and a good ladder rings true, whether of
wood or steel or aluminum. It is said that it is bad luck to
walk under a ladder. But think of me, poor ladder! With me,
one can achieve heights or plumb depths; cross chasms; pick
apples, rescue cats, pluck folk from burning tenements; elope
with the girl next door. One can shop the top shelf, locate
a volume, study a beehive; storm fortresses; paint eaves;
commence repairs. Put me together with a hook and a chas-
sis, add a bell, and you have a red, red fire engine. So take
the next step, or rung: buy me, carry me home, and watch
me expand with happiness.

The Welcome

Do you wish to immigrate to my heart? Where are your papers? What are your purposes?

Are you lost? Are you broken? Come to the chamber of my heart for safety. Remember the old country. I was not there. I was waiting for you here.

Do you wish to be naturalized in my arms? Let me instruct you in the new tongue. Tread softly; Death too first makes inquiry, then shows the way.

Come, pledge allegiance to my tattered proud flag. Here, and here only, the streets are paved with gold.

Typewriter

I am a typewriter. Practically an antique. Before I pass into oblivion, let me assert myself; so you may come to honor, in passing, the machine that has been a good companion to writers. Now is the time for all good men to come to the aid of their typewriters. In my sculpted black steel body I house as zany a bunch of characters as any you might want to meet, from A to Z; plus enough signs, symbols, and numbers to read the future without animal entrails. I get good character references (this being one of them), despite the fact that I am occasionally shiftless. Upper or lower, I'm a case in point. If you keep tabs on me, you'll find that I'm usually all keyed up. Nevertheless I travel in style, by carriage, to the margins of existence. Feed me the old papyrus; I will produce literature (or camp or trash or tractate). Carbon paper, with whom I always had an uneasy relationship, has gone the way of the quill pen. Keep my platen clean, and I'll always be on a roll. Stop by for a drink at my Space Bar (far out); try an ink cocktail, otherwise known as a Typewriter Mary. Scotch whiskey will clean my keys and your whistle. Rubbing alcohol makes a good (but lethal) chaser, and will also clean *your* keys. Apply the proper dosage of White-Out, and I stand corrected. I bring back the glorious era of cut-and-paste, when typewriters were typewriters. Do you recollect my purposeful clatter at all hours? After many strikes, or blows, I proudly display my campaign ribbon. Although I'm old fashioned, I may still be your type, writer. They say I go for a song now. I always did. How about for a prose poem?

14

Cricket

The green bear was vacationing in the mountains. He saw a cricket. The cricket was ten feet tall. The green bear said, "Let me get out of here!" The cricket replied, "Sir, life is an endless book. When you and I are long covered over, little will it matter that I stood several handstands above you. You, sir, are the cricket, and I am the green bear."

The cricket's words struck terror in the green bear's heart. He returned to his place of birth to trace his lineage as a green bear. In an archive he found that an uncle had misrepresented himself when running for office; that in fact he came from a long line of impostors; and that brute force was required to change the metaphor.

In truth it was absolutes that did him in. For the green bear was no better and no worse than the rest of us.

And he came back and slew the cricket without fanfare. This adventure proves that the green bear is essential to our economy and our way of life. God bless!

"In the Fullness of Time"

"In the fullness of time," he thought, he sought restitution for the scandal of his life—his fly-by-night childhood. He slowed down like a slow-poke and breathed air into the tired old catechism. He wrote down every word and thought that blazed through his head. His arms and legs deteriorated, but his trunk was intact, and he could still make love.

This tired old soldier put together the many pieces of his existence, until the completed puzzle showed a great bear, a green one, silhouetted against the skyline.

He pondered the meaning of it all: his shiftless countenance, the crate in which he arrived, the vilification of his near-ancestors. He stood tall and bright in the shadow of the clock. His hands pointed where the clock hands pointed, "In the fullness of time."

A Reincarnation

The green bear died, and came back to life as a green bear, not as a worm or a table or a chair or anything else.

He looked around him and said, "Everything looks as it did, except for one thing: a huge patch of my flesh is stuck to the radiator over there. How did I come to be wounded? Why am I incomplete?"

A voice said: "You, sir, have offended the gods, such as they are, having forsaken the clay from which you sprang. You are left torn and abandoned in your new life." "Sir," replied the green bear, "nought that you can say will make a difference. The tides are won, and the steadfast are uproarious. The green bear is sleepless; he lives again."

Then the green bear smiled, as much as a bear can be said to smile, and looked before him at a distance of many handsprings. The underpinnings were narrow, but he stood dusty and stodgy in his new life, almost an advertisement for a cigar.

Missing Person

I am a missing person. The last time I saw myself was in the mirror of a motel room in Needles, NM, four years ago. I looked awful. I shaved, showered, and walked out into the broad sunlit square—where I was gunned down by an agoraphobic New Mexican with a bristly beard and (I'm told) whiskey breath. I was rushed to a hospital and have been missing ever since.

I am a missing person. I miss love and laughter and achievement. I miss health and fame, fortune and advancement. I bear no name, no address, no country, no countryman; no landsman and no paladin.

I miss a mother and a father, my old girlfriends, even my old dogs and cats. I miss my youth, my sanity, my sense of well-being, my worldly riches. The other night I saw myself in blackest night. If I could find my identity I would throw it off a rooftop. I put the lie to such statements as, "You cannot miss what you never had." I miss meaningful employment; marital bliss; offspring; religion. The list of how I am missing is practically endless. I am misanthropic, misled, miscreant, demystified; mythopoeic and metropolitan. In dreams, when I go to shoot my enemy, I miss.

I am a missing person. I have certain clues as to my whereabouts: a button, a piece of bitumen, a birthmark; certain tastes and predilections. I am also the subject of several reported sightings. An old lady in Wichita spotted a drunken sailor in her garden—me? A Tucson bus driver narrowly missed hitting a green-haired pedestrian—me? Such sightings have been vigorously denied by the authorities. They say, "Proof is missing."

I am a missing person. To qualify for the reward, you must be instrumental in making a positive identification. You may find me, but if I do not know who I am, I may still be missing.

If you tell me who I am, I will spit in your eye.

Panama

He wore his panama everywhere. He wore it in the shower, he wore it to cure a toothache, he waved it to the horses on parade, and he doffed it to the ladies. He pulled his panama down when he played a gunslinger; he wore it high when he emulated a priest. He pursued it when the wind took it away. He never kept his panama in its round box because he wore it to sleep.

One day the man from Panama came. He reclaimed the hat and left our man bereft. Until he found a hatmaker who made him another panama, with glee. He continued making his rounds, doffing and donning his hat.

They carried him to his grave on a pallet, wearing his panama. This is vintage panama. This is a eulogy.

Pilgrim

The family stood in the house of the church. The church stood in the heartland of a maze. A pilgrim came and brought with him the plague. So he got a leg up on the grave, and grew tiresome to the officials. And the pilgrim dwindled, until he was no more than a speck of dust on a shoe. And he caused to be made an inquiry; and the inquiry found him to be guilty of legerdemain. So he hoofed it to the battlefield, where he grew graceful in the emprise. And beautiful women flocked to adore him. And he grew old in a maze, where the music failed him, and he grew wild and contentious.

Seasons

The leaves were falling, and the green bear was in a rout. The temperature was dropping, and the green bear was aging. Soon the snow would fall, and the green bear would fall also—"to sleep, perchance to dream." He deceived himself no longer: the garish summer was over, the vigor of it spent. Never again would he have to take on the burden of the double, that bilious counterpart who raised his fearsome head many times. So the green bear softened towards midwinter, and grew old in his ageless season.

Tomfoolery

The green bear was remotely possible. His tomfoolery offended all but the comatose. What a satchel he carried around with him! Full of poems, stories, old sayings; combs and cornucopia; piecework and legendaria. He halted at the edge of the known world, and reminisced.

He saw cloudy caverns spewing volcanic ash; he saw weakfish and brook trout in a kettle; he said hocus-pocus over the hors d'oeuvres, and eyed suspiciously the gendarmerie; as he swept up his sayings in a pork barrel, priding himself on the end of his discipleship. This is a plug for the doppelganger.

Antelope School

The green bear was going to antelope school. The first thing he learned was, never shout at an antelope. And the second thing was, that the antelope was an unquiet creature, who lived on the edge of the forest, and was easily misled. The green bear learned many other things about this fabulous animal, but most of all, that it could not elope with an ant; furthermore, that it poked its head in where it was not wanted; and third that its fine tongue was useful for sealing envelopes.

Antelope school was rigorous. Graduates were required to sing the praises of the creature as they went about their tasks in forestry or ministry. Above all, as the green bear soon learned, once you have an antelope you have a polonaise, and once you have a polonaise you have two antelopes, male and female, and so on until the eternity of antelopes is achieved, next door to the eternity for green bears; towards which our green bear yearned, and was reconciled.

Shoe

Once upon a time there was a man who fell off a shoe. He landed in the drink. He could not swim, so he grabbed hold of a shoelace and hung on. Word was abroad that he needed help.

He pushed one foot then the other against the tide, and threatened to dissolve. So blissfully he receded into the dangerous years, where wide-eyed he trod water in the garden of the goddess. Slowly, ever so slowly, the spell wore off; until at last he could remount the shoe. He waved goodbye to his salad days, and strode where the shoe strode, by a thread; past a yellow box containing truth, however puerile.

Time Poem

How many watches on watchbands does it take to tell the exact time? I do not wish to be early, and I do not wish to be late.

If I ask that question of passers-by, they will surely think I am mad.

If I call for the correct time, how will I know I am not dreaming? If my call is monitored by extraterrestrial beings, is all of time compromised? If I conclude that I am awake, how can I get where I am going without fresh obsessions and delusions?

Is there an autumnal flow from outer space, a pulse from the atomic clock, a reading done in extreme motion? Is jet time the same from Mandalay to the Taj Mahal? Will I be called on the carpet to explain time to a metronome? Are the rigors of the just concomitant with exile? Is time a decade that cannot be stopped? A dynamo that powers every black-jack game in the world? What must I do to station myself among the just? I do not wish to be early, and I do not wish to be late.

Varlet

Varlet? What the devil is a varlet? Is a varlet a velvet cousin of the ocelot? I don't think so. Is it something svelte? Can I find one on a veldt? In a weltanschauung? Is a varlet someone who shines your shoes, and presses your pants? I don't think so.

Is a varlet a larva? Or more likely a vulva? Is a varlet small and furry, like a hamster? Or lean and hungry, like a varmint? Is it something growing purple in your garden, or scarlet on your trellis? Varlet? What the devil is a varlet? Is it anything, anything at all, like a rivulet? I think it is something virulent, virulent.

Tourniquet

Ah! What lightning is this? What osprey? What tangle-wood?

In severing himself from his past, the green bear sliced through an artery. The medicos wondered that he was still alive. They gathered 'round and proposed this remedy and that. The green bear was bleeding to death.

The green bear made a tourniquet out of one of his poems, and stopped the bleeding. Now he limped along, slowly, this scrivener, sovereign of the behest; so that he lived to be as old as the cities, while piping down the woodlands wild, piping down the everglades; and all the time his great friend Lycidas was lost at sea. So be it; in the altitudes one cannot always predict the freshets; in a satrap one cannot be sure of the grail; in a fleecing, beware, as he shouldered the bricks like a hod carrier. These were the pyrotechnics of a green bear, lost in the curvature of the earth.

The Little Pastor

In the old country the little pastor used to take care of the ships. But once he fell into a deep sleep. Then wolves came and ate all the ships. So the scavengers descended.

It was desert in the old country, it was brushfires and dust-bowls. It was whiplash too, as you might expect. So in the furthest valley the laborers saw a forest with trees and sunshine, an orderly allotment of greens. Now this forest bordered the desert and the desert bordered the sun; and the old country was the land of sun and coffee and peach trees. And the little pastor woke from his sleep of centuries. He cried, "Listen to me! I was amazed before you! I froze and came back in time, and wept over the eclipse."

So was the little pastor made guardian of the land beyond the mountains. For the old country was uninhabitable for the little pastor, who could not, after so many years, protect the ships.

Back from Exile

The green bear came back from exile; exiled not from his homeland but from the crossroads of his imagination.

He tidied things up a bit, then strolled onto the busy, merry street. Imagine his surprise when he ran into his old comrade-in-exile, Jules. Jules, or Julie as he liked to be called, was punch-drunk with new life. Together they forged a remarkable team: macabre but combustible, with fire in their eyes. So the green bear, Jules, and the rest took to the streets in the hi-ho of their heyday, bearing their trophy aloft, a samovar. Quiz me no more. These were their exploits. This was their escapade. These were their permutations.

Point of No Return

The green bear reached the point of no return. He named his executors and stepped wide-eyed into the future. He fairly flew with rage and respite, and rolled his eyes over the entitlement. Tethered to the past he was impotent; set free, he was munificent. The chariot that bore him said, in red letters, "Right-Righteous." And the tombstone they quarried for him called him "Sane." So he wolfed down the last of the statutes and proceeded along the dewy-eyed course of wet weather; and rejoined his comrades in the great encyclical. So he stood up for the oddments of his life, as by a field planted with tall clover, or cotton. And it was wet weather, alright, for the Right-Righteous, at the point of no return; a freshet, a Danube.

Advice

"Whatever you do," said the green bear, "don't step on your own cock."

In the variegated landscape it seemed simple advice, and it made sense. For the green bear was expert at self-sabotage, accidental and deliberate; having been through it all, by the numbers, so that the outcome was predictable.

On the doorstep of his demise he sought recognition for his endgame—magisterial, folksome, clairvoyant. He laughed it up and parsed his acrimony, by the music; by the selfsame enterprise as made the great emporium in the sky.

He papered-over the darkness with his landscape. His epitaph read, "Here lies the green bear, who learned, finally, to not step on his own cock."

Bluestocking

By mudflats, see? If you look south you'll see the green bear, traipsing along, oblivious, caught up in his poem-for-a-day. Now, that's not right, green bear: to stay off by yourself and not share yourself with the gentry! And not mix with the populace! Surely you see the wrong of that. And at once you must know this: we all love you, green bear, so keep on traipsing on, and we'll play a Bob Dylan record for you, just to get you in the mood for romance. See? Yonder? On the other side? A bluestocking, waiting for you. With her hair all up in rollers, but her heart in the right place. A worthy mate to the emulous green bear. A motif, if you like, and a guy-wire; if you look south; far away; by mudflats, see?

Skydiver

In the clay abstract it was winsome for the skydiver. So it befell. So in the short run he sped, in the long run he grieved. Over and over the voluptuous tune played, and the plague befell, as the warranty ceased in the abstract. So as from a great height he spied. And the earth was alive with vehicles and common men. And the cliffhanger stole the show. Until at length it was time again for the skydiver to suit up.

And so befell the winsome tale of a skydiver, unfinished, like the onset of fever. So he clapped his hand to his brow and swore vengeance against the cattle barons. And his rainbow prevailed. And in the clay abstract it was mightily forsooth, a chapbook, a dusty spectrum, a peregrination.

27 and 1/2

The green bear was shopping the world's largest department store. The elevator stopped, mysteriously, at Floor 27 and 1/2. He decided to get off.

He saw the many wares of Floor 27 and 1/2. He saw fraternity paddles and loggerheads; bottled zephyrs and antique dumpsters; cigar store Indians and dynamite headlines. The clerks all wore regulation army uniforms—of the Martian army. On sale were Love and Happiness, Achievement and Gregariousness, all at 27 and 1/2 price.

The green bear was a second-story man but not a second-hand man. So he rejected the bargains and opted instead for trifles from the dustbin, like bustards and flits. This was his adventure in the Celestial Flea Market of the 27 and 1/2 Floor.

A Brace of Firearms

The green bear owned a brace of fine pistols. They were blue-black, matched, and beautifully engraved, with rosewood grips. Wherever the green bear went, the brace in their satin-lined presentation box went with him.

One day, as he was meandering down a trail, he saw a covey of doves burst into the sky. A pride of lions stood at the end of his path, and a flock of starlings sailed in with a bevy of quail. A pack of wolves witnessed it all, while a pair of antique antelope watched from a distance. A bunch of hyenas laughed it up. A swarm of honeybees and a nest of vipers and a throng of other creatures completed the scene. All of this occurred beside a stand of trees: at an unknown hour of the day, on a passionate day of the week, in a month of exile.

The green bear was glad he had a brace with which to defend himself. Since there was only one of him, he deserved a brace of pistols to fight a pride of lions. Better than brickbats, any day!

Who I Am

I am—young, old, traditional and original; brave, coward-
ly, stupid, intelligent; and, to quote Geoffrey on himself,
"very good/bad/naughty/evil/pure and excellent." I am slow,
fast, aging, handsome; mad, sane, lonely, independent. I am
fearful and bold. I am I, and many I's.

I am all these things and more. I am mythic and protean.
In the sourdough of my creation, I was destined to be the
dug-out of my dreams: sent downstream, rudderless, stirred
by the reeds and the water lilies, to a makeshift harbor and a
jerrybuilt boathouse, wherein the past labors to be renamed,
and damned was the middle of the journey.

Three

The moth-eaten old centaur paid his respects to the lobbyists, then sashayed to a meeting with his counterpart, a unicorn. The unicorn was in a dusty mood. He covered himself with a blanket against prying eyes, and postponed his filibuster. Meanwhile, robust, an antelope, with his stubbed toe, approached the clearing where the centaur and the unicorn stood troubling each other. Suddenly and without warning the heavens opened up and a storm broke upon the antelope, the centaur, and the unicorn. Only the unreal survived. That is why, today, all you see are centaurs and unicorns; the antelope was too real to stay unmarried forever.

Now the antelope lives in a little square box on the outskirts of the forest. The centaur and the unicorn range over the dark forest and sniff at the coming storm. What's most real about centaurs and unicorns is that they are never seen during storms because there is no one outside to see them. I think this is the case; I hope, I hope.

Parade

One day the skinniest boys in town decided to dress up like grown men. They wore paisley four-in-hands, and three-piece readymade suits, dark blue with pinstripes, with a carnation in the lapel. They wore dark shoes and socks, like conscripts. They wore rings on their fingers of gold and semi-precious stones, like gondoliers. They hid their skinniness with great wads of paper.

They wore monogrammed Oxford shirts with French cuffs and magic cufflinks, and bowler hats like those worn by dignitaries at a ceasefire. They carried tooled leather briefcases. They wore pine-scented cologne and carried a pine branch. Last but not least, they wore trench coats big enough to conceal a broadsword. The townspeople lined the streets. The skinniest boys in town were on parade. Three cheers for their habiliments!

Mudflats

The green bear was staked out at the mudflats. It was roseate. It was a kind of chalet. It was the great divide.

His bear-sense told him it was crucial for him to meet the chandler. Where was the chandler? Lost in the necropolis. Where was the necropolis? In the substation of cities. A hundred others reached out of the rodeo, and signed up for the trepidation.

This was the green bear's crusade. It was no sleepwalk of the imagination, no covetousness of the reprieve; nor any—wide-eyed—enlightenment. Instead he did a somersault and fine-tuned his mastery, abracadabra. Whoa! What a stumble-bum!

Nepenthe

Apprehend this, Nepenthe: Is your achievement to posit the take? Are you classless, love? What egg is your grain?

Have you sat there for sunny centuries with your spoon in your mouth, waiting for the old Scrooge of the heartlands to whet his words on the keyboard?

A prism it was, to supersede the autonomous; a misericord, slapdash at the end, like a ransomed boat, a seasoned bowl, a boatman.

In the rubble of a brig called the Typhoon, old geezer, the Naiads are singing in the breeze. It is their birthday, Nepenthe, and you have flung them off like a cape; these apples of the sea, these apples of the main.

Coffee

Today I have been to three different coffeehouses in the Village, and I have reached the sixth level of enlightenment: I know that everything is coffee.

People are coffee, books are coffee, buildings are coffee; all, all is coffee. I am a fugitive from a coffeehouse. I am forgetful of the most basic things, with one exception: I know we live in a coffee universe. Even here in New York. Even in Tierra del Fuego. Even in the ghost-ridden forests of Gibralt, or that cornerstone of necromancy, the Marshall Islands; all, all is coffee for the gourmand.

Salute the freshest brew this side of Alfoxden! I am become a holy man.

The Box

In the box there were wonderful examples of folded paper and cheesecloth. There were caraway seeds too. And there was peat. Best of all, there were staples of the artifact, and a scrubbed-down version of the icon that had tempered so many lives. The box was big enough to sit on, and that he did, on the median strip, while the traffic passed around him. In his leisure time he bore witness. But sitting on the box containing folded paper and cheesecloth was his heyday, for he was indeed a billy goat, and could eat the box and everything in it, and some masonry as well. And so he fell, an emissary of the horizon, in high time for the dragon.

The One True Believer

The one true believer was scaling the heights, when his windlass broke and he sailed back into the ice cliffs. Although he perished, his pack was not spoiled; so that a young protégé could take up where he left off.

Digging into the cliff with his mountaineer boots, the young climber kept his eye on the goal, the lofty, cloudy peaks. But since he was not a true believer, like his forerunner, the young man turned to the arts for surprises. Eventually he became a troubadour. Driven by the past, he strolled in the wake of the death of the one true believer. Never question a father's antics; instead go sauntering into the future, onto the society pages of poetry.

A Reunion

The choirmaster was walking down the street, minding his
own business, when a teacup salesman approached him.
"Sir," said the salesman, "these are the finest teacups avail-
able anywhere. Put them together with any saucers you may
have lying about the house, and you will be ready for high
tea."

The choirmaster replied, "Sir, permit me to ask, what part
of the country are you from?"

"North by northwest," said the teacup salesman; "or, if you
wish, south by northwest. Why, then, do you ask?"

"Well," replied the choirmaster, "once upon a time I saved
the life of a young teacup salesman, and I thought, sir, it
might have been you." So the two embraced; and though he
sold no more teacups that day, the salesman earned a place
in history by befriending the choirmaster, who was destined
for great things. It was a grand evening; and to celebrate
they smashed not a few teacups. But it was like a marriage,
in that they labored to bring forth this poem, in its style, to-
gether with its punctuation: like a homily; or indeed like a
cypress.

On the Bridge

On the bridge he spoke of the lesson. On the bridge looking down at the water he saw the plankton. But under it all was earth, then liquid fire, then a hard core of smoky rock.

So he stood on this bastion overlooking the dustbowl of the tides of the ocean. On the bridge he performed expertly a concert in his mind. Under the bridge flowed hastily the expectant waters. It was not a dead canal.

In this colloquy of darkness he succumbed to the melancholy of the years, timing his minstrelsy to the gait of the ocean triremes. On the hearth of the bridge he carved his vagrancy. On the stallion robust of the bridge he grappled the suspension.

Under the bridge there flowed like bourbon the delicious waters of the ice. Over the bridge flowed the sky, with its rivers and portals. The bridge was the only stationary thing for miles.

Rock

I am a rock. Curved, smooth, not heavy. Grey. Covered
with moss or lichen. Concealing soil and sometimes ants and
other insects. People stub their toes on me. People hurl me
at other people, at cars, at buses and buildings; but I am
hurled back. Few folk are as steady as I. I cannot move but
am easily moved. When dropped I'm heavy enough to bruise
a foot. Inside me is locked—more rock; sometimes gold and
other precious metals; sometimes fossils of strange creatures.
Arrange me in a circle and you have the makings of a camp-
fire. Pile me on top of enough others like me, and you have a
cairn. Expand the cairn to the right or left, cement the inter-
stices, and you have a mighty Wall. My kin come in all
shapes and sizes. I honor Gibraltar as my granddad. Launch
big brothers of mine from catapults, and you can lay siege to
the strongest town. Inscribe me at the outset of construction,
and you have a proud cornerstone. Citadels are my forte. My
opposite number is called "A Hard Place." Ships at sea be-
ware of me; and mariner, beware the Sirens of the rock. As-
sembled in megaliths on Salisbury Plain are my fellows the
stones of Stonehenge, one of the mysteries of the universe.
So pray, do not mock me; put stock in me. And that's no
crock.

Born in England

I know him! I know that boy! He was born in England, in England raised up. And now he is here—with a kind of trial on his lips, a truth; but what to say, and whom to say it to?

This boy was born in England. His every move attests to that fact. For he is, certain, a walking Big Ben, tall, with crazy hands; and the bridge of his nose is London Bridge; and his hatless head is the Houses of Parliament.

In a dark, in a dark, in a dark time, the boy was born in England, and went down to London, and covered up his body with English clothes, and, walking, was a suited Burberry. Now this boy was soon a man. And under the table his transactions failed; and above board they succeeded—so that he came to America, where, hand over ironclad fist, he exacted his first fistful of dollars.

This boy was born in England. How sad. How uncertain. Wherever he was born, I am sure a visitor will say, How odd! How frightening!

Bird of Paradise

The green bear was situated on a remote point of the globe. To the east was Tangiers, to the south was Marrakesh; north was Wales, and west was Aberdeen. No one could find him here. He was not on any proper map.

He had mixed feelings. On the one hand he treasured his anonymity; on the other, he wanted to be found. It so happened that a bird of paradise flew by that very instant, inspiring the green bear to try out wings. But, like Icarus, the green bear flew too close to the sun; his wings melted, and he fell to earth.

It was only a fortnight's journey to the source of all oceans, so he sometimes walked, sometimes swam, in the desired direction. On his way he met the bird of paradise again. The bird perched on his shoulder, and said: "Sir, I know how you must feel—for I too am homeless, having lost my nominal homeland aeons ago. Now I go by the winds, by the aromas of forests, by the strength of cataracts. I can fly; but you, sir, can walk and lope and run. I admonish you: take up the flag of the fallen guidon, and advance manfully into the future."

Suddenly the bird had flown. Moved, the green bear felt his fears cascade from him like the waters. And wherever he stood, on dry land, he stood alone.

A Meeting

At long last the choirmaster met the costermonger. They had sought each other for years, always almost meeting, five minutes too early or too late.

The choirmaster said, "I harbor no grudges against you, though you have eluded me all these years." The costermonger replied, "I do not doubt your sincerity. But, friend, I would not trust you at a stonesthrow."

So began their slow duel. And so they fought, implacable foes, in hand-to-hand combat, each with an Excalibur, clashing: until at length the sun went down, and the moon climbed the horizon, to shed its light on all displaced choirmasters and costermongers. And they shook hands and fled, one past the other, into the land of snow and ice, past the tents of the Maccabees; huddling in the rainforests, decamped among the territories, crucified in the rock.

Flight

Birds fly. Astonishing. Birds of a feather fly. Rare birds fly. Captive birds do not fly. Dead and gone birds will never fly again. To conjugate all instances in which a bird may or may not fly gives insight into the problems of a receding century. For wheresoever flight has had its name, the great men of the circuses have proved that men too can fly, and women.

Witness the skill and derring-do of the trapeze artists. They fly without wings, and capture each other to save each other. Champions of the air, their glidepaths must always coincide. For it is not wisdom that determines the height of an empty fall, or the flick of a horse's mane in the circle below. Ah, would that I too could fly, and so affably enter my later years. When I think of the future, my hands curl into fists, as if to grip the bar of a trapeze.

Love Poem

This is a poem about love; but so soft, you can hear your shoes crinkle. I took a spoon and measured out the coffee of love. I added the cream of love and the sugar of love. I stirred and all was well, and I drank. And there came to me a wondrous vision: the coffee growers of the world forgathered, and love was the unannounced guest. And there I spilled the beans and declared my love.

I strode confidently to the bridge that unites two worlds. I drank a demitasse, and reveled in cappuccino. And I was saved.

The Key

Once upon a time there was a man who had a magic key. The key would unlock any door in the universe. The man stayed home always in order to protect his magic key. One day a sprite came to him and said, "I am here for you. There is no one more beautiful than I in the universe. Give me your magic key and I will be your lover forever."

But the man would not part with his key. Instead he only guarded it more closely, never even emerging from the room where he kept the key.

One night not long thereafter, a ghost visited the man. The ghost said, "Give me the key and I will punish all your enemies for you, even the enemies of your childhood."

But the man would not be swayed. Instead he guarded the key ever more closely, not even permitting himself to rise from the chair where the key was hid.

And soon he had another visitor. The visitor was an alien from outer space. The alien said to the man, "Only give me your key, and I will teach you the principles of time travel. You will be master of time past, time present, and time future. You will make a huge fortune and be the envy of all mankind."

But the man with the key would have none of this. O foolish man, don't you realize you can never use your magic key unless you give up guarding it in a little room?

Watson

Suddenly the green bear knew who he was. Sudden he grew big with knowledge.

He knew he was big, like the mountains. He knew he was fair, like the skies. And he knew he was green, like the earth. What he did not know was his name. Therefore the other animals gave him a name. It was Watson, as in Sherlock Holmes; it was Lantern, which you can see for miles; and it was Limerick, all down a distance to the seat of language, at the very edge of civilization.

But the green bear's emotions were frozen over, glacial. Therefore he saw himself as if from afar, cavorting with the polar bears—an improvement over his old life as a solitary wanderer of the Adirondack. A way to go, for Watson, Lantern, Limerick, the green bear, in these ribald, pesky times.

Shuteye

The green bear was just getting some shuteye, when the sky fell. The caliph beckoned him to his tent. "Green bear," he said, "interpret this omen. Why has the sky fallen, and what does it portend?"

The green bear rubbed his sleepy eyes and proceeded to discourse: "Once, in the temple, the plenary foe waxed strong. The sun and the moon were cast out as so much rubble. The shepherd plied his wherewithal, and the helpmeet added frost to the fire. Now has the sky fallen, as a premonition of the ascendancy of the littlest gods. Beware, for you are one of them."

So the caliph transferred his miter and his cloak of office to the green bear, who sat forevermore at the right hand of the god of ligaments and bones. It was a glamorous job, but his thoughts were always elsewhere: if not on shuteye, then subterfuge.

A Mystery

It was some time before he could tell where he was. He poked around. Here was a kitchen sink. Here was a telephone. And here was a big splash of paint on the wall, still wet and sticky.

He attempted to orient himself, but it was almost pitch black and he could not find a light switch. So he sat down on a soft cushion. He started to reminisce. "This is where I got shot." "This is where I turned into a tiger."

Now the choirmaster entered. The protagonist could hear the footsteps and the choirmaster's heavy breathing. Suddenly he jumped up from the cushion and attacked the choirmaster. The choirmaster hit him over the head with his baton case.

The choirmaster found the light switch and surveyed the damage. He said, "It will take years to make all this right again. What do you do with a life that is a disaster? Do you stay put? Do you argue? Do you get drunk?" The choirmaster aged rapidly, then fell to the floor freezing. Suddenly the heavens opened up and showered the scene with pink rain. And the grief departed, and the nuggets of sugar sweetened the tooth of the adversaries.

Trust Me

Trust me. Milk and cookies are good for you. They put bones on your marshmallows.

Once upon a time I ate my way out of house and home. I could not keep my hands off the cherries and grapes and what have you. I was led from my premises by a trained dog on a leash, and turned over to the Shakespearians.

I got around all right after that, with the shield of the Shakespearians on my forehead; but never did I lose my appetite for milk and cookies. You would not either, if you were a Shakespearian, or wore buskins. Not for a minute. Trust me.

Statistics

What is the copulation of the United States? I will tell you. There are four in Nebraska, seven in San Diego, and a duet in Alaska. This, then, is the copulation of the United States, at entry level, sea level, and mountain level, respectively.

There is, in this great land of ours, a serious threat of over-copulation. Citizens are urged to practice insolence, and to refrain from—or practice a safe form of—hex. Lest there be any further hex in our notable history, let there be over-and-under capitulation exclusively. There is a whole world to feed!

To Be Part of a House

I am a house. Love me, I keep you warm in winter, cool in summer. Love me, love my parts.

To be a part of a house is wonderful. Take me, for example: I am a roof; I get the shingles bad, but I keep out the rain. Or me—I'm a window; through me the world glares, but my tenants glare back; I don't fool any of them for a minute, they can see right through me. The whole thing is a pane. As a window I'm an open and shut case, like my neighbor the door. Or look, I'm a hardwood floor: dance upon me, wax me often, love my parquetry.

Love me, I'm a kitchen. I cook up the right stuff: boil the water, broil the steak, heat the beans. Before me you had to do those things in a fireplace; that was nice; I like those old kitchens, my ancestors. I am where the bacon is brought when Papa Bear brings it home. I am where the bread that has been won is stashed. Do you have a beef, a bone to pick, a steak in the proceedings? I'm here. I am where the ovenbird is a turkey, not a songster. I am where the tea is brewed and the brew is Bud; where the ice cream is fudged; where the budget is frugal; where the cupboards are as clapboards. I bridle to say so, but I am a kind of far-west kitchen, complete with ten-gallon hat for measuring, and my own rendition of "Home, Home on the Range."

I'm a bedroom. I'm great for rest, sleep, privacy; for premarital heaven, marital coma, postmarital bliss. On my big brass bed my image remains untarnished. My nightstand has stood me in good stead for innumerable one-night stands.

I'm a bathroom. Not a good place for pipe dreams, since I run hot and cold. My mirror displays a reflective nature, whilst my washstand looks as if it may or may not hold water or stand on its own two feet. Sometimes I flush with embarrassment or pride. Sometimes my shower stalls, or my sink runs over. And sometimes my tenant's luck just runs out, and he Takes a Bath or Gets Soaked without ever coming near me.

I am a living room. With my sofas covered by covers covering covers, I am couched in terms more appropriate to horseplay than to serious company. My lamp shades are not a shade too light or too dark. My bay window admits light, sheds light, and keeps the world at bay. And it will be curtains for someone at the end of this little drama if he does not put a doily behind his head when he sits here. My love seat in green satin is so elegant that no one dares sit on it. What is more pitiable than an unloved love seat? My side chairs, on the other hand, are no less elegant than my side tables; and sidekicks love to sit on side chairs and drink coffee from side tables. Only occasionally are my occasional tables tables; the rest of the time they are stabiles. My ancient Victrola is as compelling as its master's voice. Would that the language of my fireplace were bright with bricks, crispy with twigs, and fluent with flame; for an unused fireplace is cold comfort. Nevertheless there is a baby grand in this room, which Mama Bear plays well enough to bring love and loss to the heart of at least one member of the household.

I am a den. Throughout the house hear me growl. I am where Papa Bear holds court, until Baby Bear shall have grown up to have his own study. See how my bookshelves embrace the splendid volumes. See how each bookend keeps up its end of the bargain. Observe the leather couch, fine for spuds of all ages. Note my handsome mahogany paneling, for when Papa Bear is in a brown study. My chair is the seat of tyranny: armed, overstuffed, and dangerously redolent of Papa Bear.

Last, but not least, I am a secret room. (Now not so secret any more.) Not even Papa Bear, who designed this, his dreamhouse, with an architect, knows of my existence. That's because I am invisible, a transparent shell into which my young tenant crawls to escape the dangers, pitfalls, and humiliations of the world; like a space suit worn in a hostile environment. I am thin and crisp as a fine poem. My inner surface is like the inside of a planetarium, with many marvels to behold by starshine. Here are thoughts and imaginings worthy of a biblical David, poet, lover, warrior, and king. Here is recovery, renewal, regeneration.

Now that you know who I am, you must take care when you approach me. Letters to deliver? Milk? Repairs called for? Sudden death to report? Come to the house on Reno, house on Reno, house on Reno Road. And to the screened porch where my young tenant reads great books and eats grapes all summer long.

And so a whole house is a barn field, but not of wild animals. And so a barn is a whole house of family, with plenty of room for parts. A house is not yet a barn; nor is a field a meadow. And so a barn is not a house afield.

Come again sometime to find out who and what else lives in this curious place.

Fortuitous

The green bear was fortuitous in the extreme. He hollowed out his cockleshell and lambasted the waves, as they sought to engulf him, the maverick waves. Fortuitously he climbed to the crow's-nest, where he sighted the stranger ship, the Pendragon. He hollered for his ship to be ready, with all its guns bristling. Sudden upon a cloud the reindeer appeared, and the shots fell short. It was Christmastime, and the green bear patched up his life with oilcloth, on the frontier, on the edge of the absolute; in a cross-carriage of the vindictive; in a cry of wonderment, beseeching. It was the miracle of the cannonade, a foxfire of the indifferent, which decimated his all-but-hollowed-out cockleshell.

Strictly Speaking

Strictly speaking, from his coign of vantage the green bear sought to initiate his acrimony; yet he sailed like brocade into the future. First he picked the flower of darkness. Then the flower of light. Then the rose of severance, apocalyptic in his speech book. Tenderly he caressed the dust covers, in the half-light, where the coin shone, the coin of acres. It was a statute that he finally settled on, brandishing the tocsin like a steamfitter. In all this he was his own guide through the sultry darkness. He stood up for green bears everywhere, though there was only one of him. In the language of the patriarchs, he was enscrolled in the book of fire, effusive, scalding, aromatic. It was his way of warming to the gentry, of flowing like foolscap through the mightiest press, the Pendragon.

David Friedman was born and raised in Washington, D.C., and was educated at Cornell (B.A.) and Columbia (M.A., English Literature). At Cornell, thanks in part to a wonderful English department, he fell in love with literature and found his lifelong dream: to become a writer and contribute to literature. He lives in New York City and teaches adult education.

Illinois Poetry Series
Laurence Lieberman, Editor

Dance Script with Electric
Ballerina
Alice Fulton (reissue, 1996)

To the Bone: New and Selected
Poems
Sydney Lea (1996)

Floating on Solitude
Dave Smith (3-volume reissue,
1996)

Bruised Paradise
Kevin Stein (1996)

Walt Whitman Bathing
David Wagoner (1996)

Rough Cut
Thomas Swiss (1997)

Paris
Jim Barnes (1997)

The Ways We Touch
Miller Williams (1997)

The Rooster Mask
Henry Hart (1998)

The Trouble-Making Finch
Len Roberts (1998)

Grazing
Ira Sadoff (1998)

Turn Thanks
Lorna Goodison (1999)

Traveling Light:
Collected and New Poems
David Wagoner (1999)

Some Jazz a While:
Collected Poems
Miller Williams (1999)

The Iron City
John Bensko (2000)

Songlines in Michaeltree: New
and Collected Poems
Michael S. Harper (2000)

Pursuit of a Wound
Sydney Lea (2000)

The Pebble: Old and New Poems
Mairi MacInnes (2000)

Chance Ransom
Kevin Stein (2000)

House of Poured-Out Waters
Jane Mead (2001)

The Silent Singer: New and
Selected Poems
Len Roberts (2001)

The Salt Hour
J. P. White (2001)

Guide to the Blue Tongue
Virgil Suárez (2002)

The House of Song
David Wagoner (2002)

X =
Stephen Berg (2002)

Arts of a Cold Sun
G. E. Murray (2003)

Barter
Ira Sadoff (2003)

The Hollow Log Lounge
R. T. Smith (2003)

In the Black Window: New and
Selected Poems
Michael Van Walleghen (2004)

A Deed to the Light
Jeanne Murray Walker (2004)

Controlling the Silver
Lorna Goodison (2005)

Good Morning and Good Night
David Wagoner (2005)

American Ghost Roses
Kevin Stein (2005)

National Poetry Series

Eroding Witness
Nathaniel Mackey (1985)
Selected by Michael S. Harper

Palladium
Alice Fulton (1986)
Selected by Mark Strand

Cities in Motion
Sylvia Moss (1987)
Selected by Derek Walcott

The Hand of God and a Few
Bright Flowers
William Olsen (1988)
Selected by David Wagoner

The Great Bird of Love
Paul Zimmer (1989)
Selected by
William Stafford

Stubborn
Roland Flint (1990)
Selected by Dave Smith

The Surface
Laura Mullen (1991)
Selected by C. K. Williams

The Dig
Lynn Emanuel (1992)
Selected by Gerald Stern

My Alexandria
Mark Doty (1993)
Selected by Philip Levine

The High Road to Taos
Martin Edmunds (1994)
Selected by Donald Hall

Theater of Animals
Samn Stockwell (1995)
Selected by Louise Glück

The Broken World
Marcus Cafagña (1996)
Selected by Yusef Komunyakaa

Nine Skies
A. V. Christie (1997)
Selected by Sandra McPherson

Lost Wax
Heather Ramsdell (1998)
Selected by James Tate

So Often the Pitcher Goes to
Water until It Breaks
Rigoberto González (1999)
Selected by Ai

Renunciation
Corey Marks (2000)
Selected by Philip Levine

Manderley
Rebecca Wolff (2001)
Selected by Robert Pinsky

Theory of Devolution
David Groff (2002)
Selected by Mark Doty

Rhythm and Booze
Julie Kane (2003)
Selected by Maxine Kumin

Shiva's Drum
Stephen Cramer (2004)
Selected by Grace Schulman

The Welcome
David Friedman (2005)
Selected by Stephen Dunn

Other Poetry Volumes

Local Men and *Domains*
James Whitehead (1987)

Her Soul beneath the Bone:
Women's Poetry on Breast
Cancer
Edited by Leatrice Lifshitz
(1988)

Days from a Dream Almanac
Dennis Tedlock (1990)

Working Classics: Poems on
Industrial Life
*Edited by Peter Oresick and
Nicholas Coles* (1990)

Hummers, Knucklers, and Slow
Curves: Contemporary Baseball
Poems
Edited by Don Johnson (1991)

The Double Reckoning of
Christopher Columbus
Barbara Helfgott Hyett (1992)

Selected Poems
Jean Garrigue (1992)

New and Selected Poems,
1962–92
Laurence Lieberman (1993)

The Dig and *Hotel Fiesta*
Lynn Emanuel (1994)

For a Living: The Poetry of Work
*Edited by Nicholas Coles and
Peter Oresick* (1995)

The Tracks We Leave: Poems on
Endangered Wildlife of North
America
Barbara Helfgott Hyett (1996)

Peasants Wake for Fellini's
Casanova and Other Poems
*Andrea Zanzotto; edited and
translated by John P. Welle and
Ruth Feldman; drawings
by Federico Fellini and
Augusto Murer* (1997)

Moon in a Mason Jar and *What
My Father Believed*
Robert Wrigley (1997)

The Wild Card: Selected Poems,
Early and Late
*Karl Shapiro; edited by
Stanley Kunitz and
David Ignatow* (1998)

Turtle, Swan and *Bethlehem in
Broad Daylight*
Mark Doty (2000)

The University of Illinois Press
is a founding member of the
Association of American University Presses.

———————————————

Composed in 10.5/13.5 New Caledonia
with ITC Cushing display
by Celia Shapland
for the University of Illinois Press
Designed by Dennis Roberts
Manufactured by Thomson-Shore, Inc.

University of Illinois Press
1325 South Oak Street
Champaign, IL 61820-6903
www.press.uillinois.edu